Horses
Graze In The
Foothills Of The
Hindu Kush

AFGHANISTAN

BY KATHRYN STEVENS

THE CHILD'S WORLD®

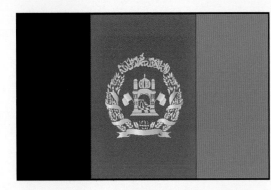

CONTENT ADVISERS

Daniel Ehnbom, Director, Center for South Asian Studies, University of Virginia, and Mehr A. Farooqi, Assistant Professor, Asian & Middle Eastern Languages and Cultures, University of Virginia

GRAPHIC DESIGN

Robert E. Bonaker / Graphic Design & Consulting Co.

PAGE PRODUCTION

The Design Lab

PHOTO RESEARCH

Dawn Friedman

PHOTO CREDITS

Cover: Webistan/Corbis; Mindaugas Kulbis/AP Wide World Photos: 11; Alexander Zemlianichenko/AP Wide World Photos: 22; Charles Rex Arbogast/AP Wide World Photos: 23; Ed Wray/AP Wide World Photos: 25; Zaheeruddin Abdullah/AP Wide World Photos: 29; Michael S. Yamashita/Corbis: 2, 8; Corbis: 9, 15, 19; Ric Ergenbright/Corbis: 10; AFP/Corbis: 16, 18, 20, 24, 27; Reuters NewMedia, Inc./Corbis: 17, 26; Webistan/Corbis: 21; Hulton Archive/Getty Images: 12, 13; Paula Bronstein/Getty Images: 14.

PROJECT COORDINATION

Editorial Directions, Inc.

Library of Congress Cataloging-in-Publication Data

Stevens, Kathryn, 1954–

Afghanistan / by Kathryn Stevens.

p. cm.

Summary: An introduction to the geography, history, plant and animal life, and social life and customs of Afghanistan.

Includes bibliographical references and index.

Contents: Where is Afghanistan?—The land -- Plants and animals—Long ago— Afghanistan today—The people—City life and country life—Schools and language— Work—Food—Pastimes—Holidays.

ISBN 1-56766-181-5 (library bound : alk. paper)

1. Afghanistan—Juvenile literature. [1. Afghanistan.] I. Title.

DS351.5.S835 2003

958.1—dc21

2002151512

Table
of
Contents

ADMIT ONE ADMIT ONE

ADMIT ONE   ADMIT ONE

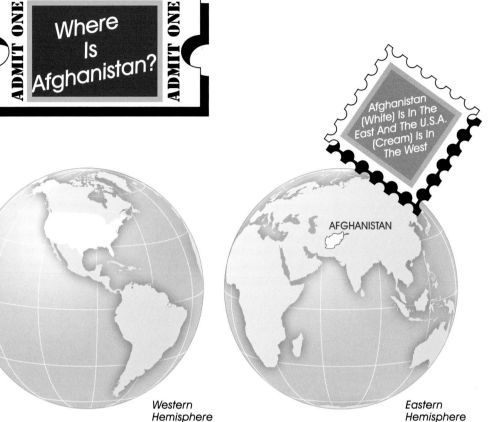

Afghanistan (White) Is In The East And The U.S.A. (Cream) Is In The West

AFGHANISTAN

Western Hemisphere

Eastern Hemisphere

If you could fly high above Earth, you would see huge land areas surrounded by blue oceans. The seven largest land areas are called continents. The largest continent is Asia. Afghanistan is in the southwestern part of Asia.

Landlocked Afghanistan is surrounded by other nations. To its west lies Iran. To its south and east, it shares a long border with Pakistan. To its north are Turkmenistan, Uzbekistan, and Tajikistan. They were once part of the Soviet Union. To the northeast, one small part of Afghanistan touches the People's Republic of China.

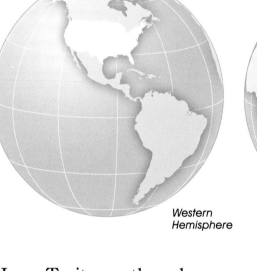

The World Shown Flat

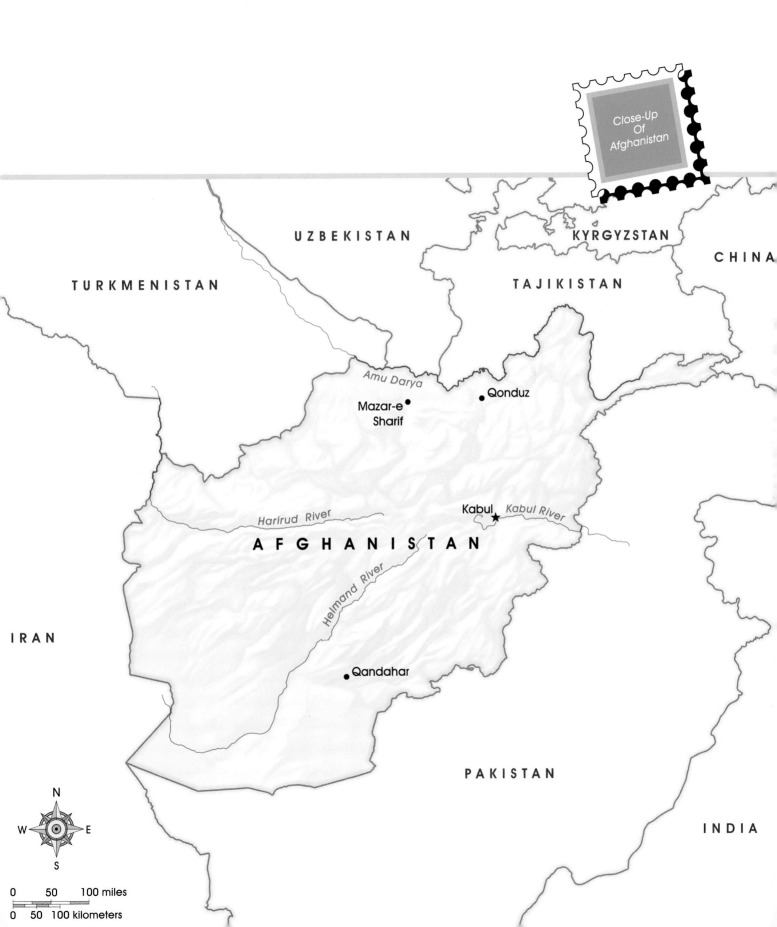

Close-Up
Of
Afghanistan

UZBEKISTAN

KYRGYZSTAN

CHINA

TURKMENISTAN

TAJIKISTAN

Amu Darya

● Mazar-e
Sharif

● Qonduz

Harirud River

Kabul ★ Kabul River

AFGHANISTAN

Helmand River

IRAN

● Qandahar

PAKISTAN

N
W   E
S

INDIA

0   50   100 miles

0   50   100 kilometers

Farmland In Jabul Saraj

Amu Darya
Mazar-e Sharif
Qonduz
Harirud River
Kabul R.
Kabul
Helmand River
Qandahar

The Land

Afghanistan's rugged central highlands, with their mountain peaks and narrow valleys, cover much of the country. The highest mountains are in the Hindu Kush, part of the Himalayan mountain range. Nowshak, Afghanistan's highest peak, is more than 24,000 feet (7,315 meters) high. North of the mountains are the northern plains and foothills. There you will see huge grasslands and rich, fertile farmland. To the south of the mountains lies the southern **plateau.** It has large, sandy deserts.

Most of Afghanistan has sunny, dry weather with only a few inches of rain every year. Winters are cold. Summers are long and hot. Higher areas are usually cooler. In the mountains, winter brings very cold temperatures, ice, and snow. Afghanistan's lower regions are warmer. In the summer, daytime temperatures in the deserts can be more than 100 degrees Fahrenheit (38 degrees Celsius).

The City Of Kabul And The Surrounding Hindu Kush Mountains

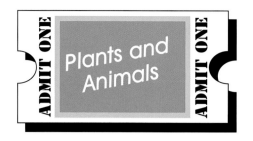

Plants and Animals

Afghanistan's rough and uneven landscape supports many kinds of plants. There are few forests. Most of the trees have been cut down and used for firewood. High mountains still have fir and pine trees and other plants that can survive the cold. Lower areas have ash, juniper, oak, poplar, and pistachio trees, as well as rose and gooseberry bushes. Farmers grow crops in some areas using water supplied by **irrigation.**

Many kinds of animals live in Afghanistan. Hunting has killed off many larger animals, including tigers. However, you may still find snow leopards, gazelles, bears, foxes, wild pigs, goats, and sheep. The region's many birds include flamingos, doves, pigeons, crows, vultures, and eagles. Rivers are home to trout, carp, sturgeon, and other fish. One-humped and two-humped camels are common. Afghan people raise them, as well as horses, cattle, sheep, and goats.

Poplar Trees Along A Dirt Road

An Afghan Boy
With A Camel

British Troops In Kabul In 1879

Mazar-e Sharif
Qonduz
Amu Darya
Harirud River
Kabul R.
Kabul
Helmond River
Qandahar

Long Ago

Humans have lived in the Afghanistan region for at least 50,000 years. The earliest people lived by hunting wild animals and collecting wild plants. About 10,000 years ago, people began raising **domesticated** animals and crops such as wheat and barley.

Afghanistan has had a difficult and violent history. Long ago, its location was important for controlling trade routes that carried silk and spices across Asia. Even after goods traveled by sea, military leaders still found the area valuable.

Many different people and governments have taken over the region. Its rough landscape and fierce Afghan fighters have made the land hard to hold onto. Among its conquerors were some of history's most famous military leaders. They include the Greek general Alexander the Great in 328 B.C., Mongolian Genghis Khan in A.D. 1219, and Tamerlane in A.D. 1370. Later, Russia and the British struggled to control the region. The British fought three wars with Afghanistan in the 1800s and early 1900s.

A Portrait Of The Conqueror Tamerlane

In addition to invaders from outside, Afghanistan's own tribes and **ethnic groups** have fought among themselves. In fact, Afghanistan did not become a single kingdom until the 1700s. Since then, fighting among different groups and political **factions** has continued.

Afghanistan Today

ADMIT ONE
ADMIT ONE

Hamid Karzai

Afghanistan's troubled history continues today. In 1973, the king was forced from power. Afghanistan began to set up a **communist** government. Many people did not want this kind of government. In 1979, they started fighting against the government. Then, in December 1979, the Soviet Union invaded Afghanistan, starting a ten-year war. The Soviets were defeated, but fighting among different Afghan groups continued.

In 2001, a different kind of war began. For years, the Taliban ruled the country. Taliban leaders followed their own strict version of the Islamic religion. They had a deep hatred for other religious beliefs or ways of life. The country became home to **terrorists** with similar views, including a wealthy Saudi Arabian named Osama bin Laden and his al-Qaeda terrorist group. Al-Qaeda attacked the United States on September 11, 2001, by flying hijacked passenger jets into buildings in New York City and Washington, D.C. The attacks killed more than 3,000 innocent people. In October 2001, the United States and other countries attacked the Taliban government for protecting bin Laden. The Taliban leaders were overthrown and replaced by a short-term government headed by President Hamid Karzai.

Afghanistan's new leaders have struggled to build a strong, secure government. One of the country's biggest problems, however, remains finding ways for people from its many cultures and regions to work together peacefully.

Soviet Troops Leaving Afghanistan In 1988

Afghan Men
Kneeling In
Prayer In
Kabul

Mazar-e
Sharif
Qonduz
Amu Darya
Harirud River
Bamiyan
Kabul R.
Helmand River
Kabul
Qandahar

Afghanistan is home to many different ethnic groups. Each group has its own culture and way of life. Many Afghans are Pashtuns. Other major groups are Tajiks, Nuristanis, and Hazaras. Smaller groups include Uzbeks, Turkmens, and Kyrgyz. The larger ethnic groups are made up of smaller tribes. Loyalties to the tribes are strong, and disagreements among tribes and ethnic groups are common.

Islam is the official religion in Afghanistan. People of the Islamic faith, or Muslims, follow beliefs laid out in the Islamic holy book, the Koran. Religious beliefs carry over into every part of daily life. There are two main versions of Islam with somewhat different beliefs and practices. Most Afghans are Sunni (SOO-nee) Muslims. The rest are Shiite (SHEE-ite) Muslims.

Three Hazara Girls In Bamiyan

In Afghanistan's cities you will find newer apartments and shops as well as old, mud-brick houses and open-air markets. Buses and automobiles move through the streets alongside camels and donkey carts. Warfare has caused heavy damage. Some city dwellers fled to places they hoped would be safer. Those who remained have faced bombings and gunfire, shortages of food and medicine, and other hardships. Rebuilding Afghanistan's cities will be a challenge.

Most of Afghanistan's people live in the country. Roads are poor, and travel is difficult.

Farmers usually live along river valleys or around water holes. There they can find water and **fertile** soil for growing crops. Their small villages have houses made of sun-dried mud bricks. Tools and farming methods are like those of long ago. Like the cities, many villages and surrounding farmlands have been damaged or destroyed by warfare.

Some Afghans are **nomads.** Nomads are people who move from place to place, raising and herding animals. They live in tents that can be taken down and carried to another site.

These Men Gather Firewood In A Village North Of Kabul

Mazar-e Sharif
Qonduz
Khwaja Bahwuin
Amu Darya
Harirud River
Helmand River
Kabul R.
Kabul
Qandahar

Men Doing Business On Market Day In Khwaja Bahwuin

Mazar-e
Sharif

Qonduz

Amu Darya

Harirud River

Helmand River

Kabul R.

Kabul

Qandahar

Children At
Alfat-Ha School
In Kabul

Schools and Language

ADMIT ONE · ADMIT ONE

Most Afghans are illiterate, which means they cannot read or write. For a number of years, Afghan children were required to attend elementary school beginning at age seven. When the Taliban took over the country, girls could no longer attend school. Wars made going to school unsafe for many children. Since the Taliban's defeat, girls have begun going to school again. Still, the nation's schools are in terrible condition, and many children are not yet able to attend. Rebuilding the school system will be an important task.

Afghanistan has two main language groups, Pashto and Dari. People in different areas speak different forms of these languages. Some people also speak Turkic, Nuristani, or Uzbek. Afghanistan's languages are written in the graceful, curved characters of Arabic.

Arabic Script On Posters Promoting Peace

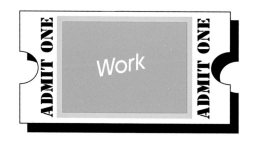

Work

Only a small amount of Afghanistan's land is fertile enough to farm. Even so, most of the country's people work as farmers. They raise animals or grow wheat, barley, corn, or cotton. They may grow sugar beets, rice, fruits, or nuts. Some workers change the crops into goods. An example of this is spinning cotton and weaving it into cloth.

Other Afghans have jobs in cities and towns, selling food or other products, or working in offices.

Afghanistan has few industries or factories. Under Taliban rule, women could not work outside the home at all. Now that the Taliban is gone, Afghan women are entering the workforce.

Many Afghans make handcrafted products to sell, including baskets, pottery, and objects made of wood, leather, and metal. Afghanistan's beautiful handmade carpets and rugs are prized throughout the world. Creating their designs requires tying a huge number of tiny knots. A single rug can take several workers months to make.

This Afghan Girl Is Weaving A Carpet

Mazar-e Sharif

Qonduz

Amu Darya

Harirud River

Kabul R.

Kabul

Helmand River

Qandahar

Boy Selling Naan, The Traditional Afghan Bread

Mazar-e Sharif
Amu Darya
Qonduz
Harirud River
Kabul R.
Kabul
Helmand River
Qandahar

Warfare has sometimes made food scarce in Afghanistan. Rice is a main food, and so is a flat bread called *naan* (NAHN). Rice is mixed with vegetables and meat to make *pilau* (pah-LAO). Meat and vegetables are placed on a skewer, or long metal rod, and grilled over charcoal to make *kebab*. *Jelabi* (JA-lay-BEE) is a fried dessert covered with sweet syrup.

A Man Drinking Tea At A Hotel In Qandahar

Many delicious fruits, including apricots, grapes, pomegranates, melons, and cherries, grow in Afghanistan. Afghans eat fruit fresh and also dried. Almonds, pistachios, and walnuts are popular, too. Afghans drink milk from cows, goats, and sheep. They also use milk to make yogurt and cheese. Strong tea is a favorite beverage. Islam forbids eating pork—the meat of pigs—or drinking alcohol.

This Girl Is Participating In An Independence Day Parade In Kabul

Spoken poetry and storytelling are an important part of Afghanistan's way of life. Some Afghan tribes pass on their histories through poems and stories. Singing, playing music, and dancing are important, too. Arts and crafts have also been part of Afghanistan's way of life.

Sports are popular in the country. Some of Afghanistan's sports have a long history. In a daring, high-speed game called *buzkashi* (BUZ-kah-SHEE), two teams on horseback try to grab the headless body of a goat or calf and carry it to a goal. This is an early form of the game of polo.

New Year's *(Nau Ruz)* falls on March 21, the first day of spring. Independence Day (August 19) marks the nation's independence from British control. Other holidays are tied to Islam, and their dates change from year to year. During the monthlong holiday of Ramadan, people fast, or do not eat, from sunrise to sunset. A feast called *Eid al-Fitr* (EED UL fitR) follows the end of Ramadan. Another important holiday honors the birth of Mohammed, the founder of Islam.

Afghanistan is a troubled land facing difficult challenges in the years ahead. Still, its people have survived hardships for thousands of years. Would you like to visit Afghanistan someday and experience its interesting land and ways of life?

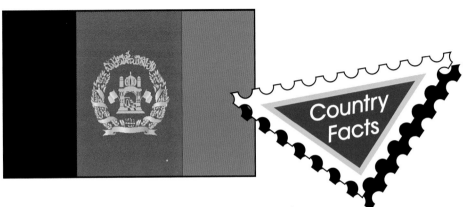

Area
About 252,000 square miles (653,000 square kilometers)—nearly as big as the state of Texas.

Population
About 26 million people. (Warfare and the large number of nomads have made the population difficult to count.)

Capital City
Kabul.

Other Important Cities
Ghazni, Herat, Jalalabad, Mazar-e Sharif, Qandahar, Qonduz.

Important Rivers
Amu Darya, Arghandab, Harirud, Helmand, Kabul, Qonduz.

Money
The Afghani, divided into 100 pule.

National Flag
Afghanistan's new flag, introduced in 2002, has black, red, and green stripes with the nation's coat of arms in the center.

Official Name
Islamic State of Afghanistan

Current Government
An interim (short-term) administration set up in June 2002 to govern until 2004.

An Afghan Nomad Family

Did You Know?

Islam controls everyday life in Muslim countries. Muslims must pray five times a day. While praying, they face east, toward the holy city of Mecca. Mecca is in the country of Saudi Arabia.

Today, most Afghans do not live as long as people in other countries. They live only into their forties. They die from disease, unsafe drinking water, poor medical care, and injuries from warfare and leftover land mines. Many Afghan children die before their fifth birthday.

In the most traditional Afghan households, adult women live in purdah (PUR-duh), which means that the only men who see them are members of their families.

Asian language sounds are difficult to write with English letters. That is why Afghan names and words often appear with different English spellings—for example, Kandahar and Qandahar.

How Do You Say?

	DARI	HOW TO SAY IT ?
hello	salaam	sah-LOHM
goodbye	kodah hafez	koh-DAH hah-FEZ
good night	shabeh kher	SHAH-beh khayr
yes	baleh	BAH-leh
no	na	NAH
please	lutfan	LUT-fun
thank you	teshakkur	teh-SHAKKUR
one	yek	YEK
two	du	DO (rhyme with two)
three	sey	SAY

Glossary

communist (KOM-yuh-nist)
A communist government controls how all of the goods and property are distributed among the country's people. Afghanistan began to set up a communist government in 1973.

domesticated (doh-MESS-tih-kay-ted)
Domesticated animals are tame and live with people rather than in the wild. Afghanistan's domesticated animals include camels, cattle, sheep, goats, and horses.

ethnic groups (ETH-nik GROUPS)
An ethnic group is a group of people who share the same culture, language, and way of life. Afghanistan has a number of ethnic groups.

factions (FAK-shuns)
Factions are groups of people who have different ideas about how things should be done. In Afghanistan, conflict between political factions has made it difficult to form a secure government.

fertile (FUR-tul)
Soil that is fertile is good for growing crops. Northern Afghanistan has some areas of fertile soil.

irrigation (eer-ih-GAY-shun)
Irrigation means using canals or other methods to bring water to dry land. Much of Afghanistan's land cannot be farmed without irrigation.

landlocked (LAND-lokd)
A landlocked country is surrounded by land, with no access to the sea. Afghanistan is landlocked.

nomads (NOH-mads)
Nomads are people who move from place to place rather than having a year-round home. Some Afghans are nomads who herd animals.

plateau (plah-TOH)
A plateau is an area of high, flat land. The southern part of Afghanistan is called the southern plateau.

terrorists (TEHR-er-ists)
Terrorists are people who use violence and threats to try to get others to do what they want. In recent years, Afghanistan has been home to terrorists.

Index

To Find Out More

BOOKS

Corona, Laurel. *Afghanistan.* Farmington Hills, Mich.: Lucent Books, 2002.

Heinrichs, Ann. *Afghanistan.* Danbury, Conn.: Children's Press, 2003.

Mirepoix, Camille, editor. *Afghanistan in Pictures.* Minneapolis: Lerner Publications, 1997.

WEB SITES

Visit our home page for lots of links about Afghanistan:

http://www.childsworld.com/links.html

Note to parents, teachers, and librarians: We routinely verify our Web links to make sure they're safe, active sites—so encourage your readers to check them out!

9/06, 1